Activities for 1 Year Olds

BY:
NICOLETTE ROUX
HEATHER KNAPP

A NOTE ABOUT SAFETY:

The activities in this book are intended to be done under adult supervision. Appropriate and reasonable caution is required at all times.

Beware when using all materials and tools suggested in this book, observe safety and caution at all times. The authors of this book disclaim all liability for any damage, mishap or injury that may occur from engaging in activities in this book.

COPYRIGHT:

DISCLAIMER:

The authors of this book are not affiliated with any of the products used or displayed in the activities and ideas of this book.

www.PowerfulMothering.com

"Play is one of the most cognitively stimulating things a child can do."

- Megan McClelland, Child Development Researcher

CONTENTS

Siblings love to join in the play with the little ones!

AUTHORS

This book is written by 2 rather different moms, each of us have 4 kids under the age of 9.

NICOLETTE ROUX

Originally from South Africa, we now live in lush Ecuador, South America.

I have 2 boys (8,6) and 2 girls (5,2). From a young age they have been really enjoying exploring and crafting with me.

A large majority of the play I do with my kids includes the taste safe concept, which basically means it is non-toxic and no harm will come to the child sticking some in their mouth and tasting it.

This idea was a must for me as my one son is on the autistic spectrum and anything sensory I would do with him would first be taste tested.

The younger girls saw this and mimicked this behavior often, and so the taste safe concept was born.

We now homeschool and enjoy educational activities on top of sensory and exploration ideas that we continue to do from when they were toddlers.

My role in the making of this book was to provide activities that a 1 year old could realistically do. I hope you enjoy these ideas and that they come in handy when you just need something to do with your child.

Other books I have created include: 99 Fine Motor Ideas, Learning with LEGO and Rice Play just to name a few.

HEATHER KNAPP

Originally from the US, we currently live in Ecuador.

My husband and I have 3 boys (8, 4 and nearly 2), and one girl (6). We are an outdoorsy and athletic family and nice year round climate, so the majority of activities that I do with my kids involve getting out of the house.

I could be considered a non- but-wanna-be-crafty mom so getting to do all of the activities in this book and become empowered to do them on my own has been awesome.

After doing these activities with my toddler and researching for this book,

I'm convinced of 4 things:

1. They really are easy, fun and quick to set up and do
2. They really do assist in brain and physical development
3. They really can be expanded and built upon as kids grow
4. Your own creativity will be inspired as well

I love how quickly my son is drawn into each activity and how we enjoy them together, and it's great watching him exercise and improve his concentration and fine motor skills, which aren't used as much when running around outside like we normally do.

I love that every activity is geared for one year olds and their development, but older kids can enjoy them and expand upon them as well (as opposed to most other books I've seen which are the other way around). The taste safe standard is also a must.

We enjoyed every activity in this book and I'm truly grateful to have discovered these simple ways to add some fun to my house and have some new tools to redirect and calm my kids when things get rowdy.

And if it gets me twenty minutes of fun with my little ones, or time to clean the kitchen while they're engaged in a worthwhile activity, it's worth it to me! I hope you enjoy each activity as much as we did!

INTRODUCTION

This book is intended for parents and caregivers who are just starting out (or even have a few kids!). It will help you build a love of activities in your child from a young age and encourage things such as fine motor skills and learning through play.

It's a collaboration between two moms with four kids each, Heather and Nicolette. The activities were chosen and developed by Nicolette, a very creative mom who has used them successfully with her children over the last several years. Heather is a busy mom who got to enjoy trying all of the activities with her son and made sure they were both engaging and fun for the toddler, and doable for even the busiest and most creatively impaired moms!

Throughout the book and for each activity, Heather shares her and her sons experiences, and talks about how doing the activities have impacted her creative abilities and time spent with her children.

We also have a section on Developmental Milestones, so you have a quick reference to know what to expect from your toddler throughout these 12 months, and we try to offer you a bit of encouragement and guidance along the way.

The idea is simplicity, accessibility and fun. Kids this age don't need expensive fancy toys, they just need opportunities to explore and experiment in a loving environment. Moms of kids this age need quick and easy ways to engage and occupy their toddlers throughout the day as they nurture them along.

The activities are simple and quick to set up, need little preparation, and use basic craft supplies and household items. Your child will love doing them over and over, with variations to keep them interesting and make them harder as you go along and your child grows.

The activities in this book are one set of tools you can use to get you through this year and beyond a little more gracefully and creatively! They can inspire you when you run out of ideas for what to do with your little one, and are also great to set up for siblings, other parents or babysitters when you need a break!

You'll enjoy seeing your child have fun while knowing they're doing a worthwhile activity, and you'll be creating a home environment that fosters interaction and imagination rather than screen time. When you start activities with your child at a young age, it will become a good habit for both of you, and you will be more likely to continue with them as your children grow, which is great for development, independent play and shared creativity.

Giving our kids the best doesn't have to break the bank. Kids this age really love just simple play, exploration, and spending time with and near you! We hope this book gives you and your toddler a healthy happy start on your learning journey together.

ROUTINE

Whether you are an extremely organized person or like to fly by the seat of your pants, having at least a little bit of routine in your home can make a big difference to a toddler. At this age, everything seems out of your toddler's control and things are changing for him every day. Even simple routines can help give him a sense of security and order.

A routine does not mean that every minute or hour of your day has to be mapped out. Routines can be as much about how we do things as much as when. When toddlers know what is expected of them, their lives are less stressful as they can participate and help and it makes them feel more accomplished.

It can also help form good habits like manners and self care, and reasonable expectations of mom and dad. Knowing that activity time comes after you finish the dishes or that snack time comes after toy cleanup (and handwashing comes before snack!) helps your child with both motivation and patience.

We can use activities to help establish routines. Even if we do them on the spur of the moment, when an activity is familiar it can be like a routine that is calming for a child. Good habits like cleanup when the activity is over are also routines that you are teaching them.

Of course, disruptions are the norm with small children in the house and we have to be flexible, but any type of regularity makes the job of both toddler and parent easier. Routines can be a powerful tool for helping manage busy lives and can grow into traditions that will help family life run smoother in the years to come.

THE LAYOUT

This book is broken into two main sections.

I. THE MILESTONES SECTION:

For your reference we've included an entire section on Developmental Milestones for One-Year-Olds, broken down into the following sections.

1. Gross Motor Skills

2. Fine Motor Skills

3. Communication Skills

4. Cognitive Skills

5. Social and Emotional Development

Each Section is further broken down into:

12, 18 and 24 Month Sections

These sections give a great overview of what your child's journey will be like over the next year.

When you understand what skills and abilities are being developed you can keep an eye on how your child is progressing, and it also can help you identify areas that your child can work on.

For example, when we started doing the activities, I (Heather) noticed right away that while my child loves to move a lot and has very strong gross motor skills, it was sometimes hard to get him to slow down and concentrate on a quieter activity and I thought that his fine motor skills should have been better than I was seeing, for his age. That was a clue for me that I need to pay a little bit more attention to those areas of his development.

Always remember that all children are unique and all grow and develop at different paces based on many factors. So don't use these milestones to compare your child to anyone, and don't freak out if they're not exactly on the timeline. Often kids this age grow and develop in spurts - they will seem to struggle with a skill for a long time, and then suddenly be good at it overnight.

What's most important is to be patient and encouraging with your child, and love and meet them where they're at. Your love and encouragement have a huge impact on your toddler's ability to learn.

Home Life:

I included this section because Milestones can seem so dry at times. They only tell half the story! This section is mom to mom, especially for first timers, to let you know that your toddler's behavior is normal! Milestones don't talk about the crying, the power struggles, the frustrations the loneliness and so on and it's always helpful when we can laugh and nod and know that we're all going through the same thing!

Helpful Hints:

We love activities, but they are just one tool in a whole range of tools that we as parents have to draw on. Hopefully this section will give you some helpful hints and ideas for managing your toddler and getting through some of those long toddler days.

Utilize Activities:

This section gives you ideas for how to incorporate activities like the ones included in this book to encourage development in each specific area.

II. THE ACTIVITY SECTION:

Here's where you will find the activities! All of the activities were provided by Nicolette and done by Heathers son Harvey (though some of the pictures feature Nicolettes 2 year old daughter who knew every activity well and enthusiastically did all of them with us!).

We've included our experiences to give you an idea of how an activity might go.

Remember that it's all about the process and having fun with your toddler - it's best to be laid back and flexible and go with their flow.

Also remember that Harvey was 18-24 months during the time of making the book and you will have a different experience with a 12-18 month old, as toddlers change so rapidly during this time.

For each activity we provide the following information:

1. Materials - Tells you the materials you will need

2. Directions - Gives you the basic directions on how to set up the activity

3. Commentary - My (Heathers) experiences and observations while doing the activities with my one year old son at Nicolettes.

4. Bonus - Describes benefits my family and I (Heather) have experienced from doing the activities at home.

5. Tips/Variations - Advice and ideas for how to do the activities with your child.

6. Bigger Kids/As They Grow - More complex options and ideas for your child as they master the activities or for older kids in the home.

7. Your Own Notes! - If your child does something really cute, you want to keep track of their development, or you and they come up with some great variations of your own, write them down so you don't forget them!

DEVELOPMENTAL MILESTONES

GROSS MOTOR SKILLS

Gross motor movements are the larger movements of the arms, legs, feet or entire body. Gross motor skills are the abilities required in order to control the large muscles of the body for walking, running, sitting, crawling, and other activities. *ref1

12 MONTHS:
At twelve months, it's all about being upright and on the go. A lot of time is spent sitting up and pulling up to standing, enjoying a new perspective while building muscle strength and coordination. These babes move by creeping, crawling, cruising the furniture and can walk pretty well while holding your hand. Some are already standing and taking those first wobbly steps solo!

18 MONTHS:
By now toddlers will walk well on their own and try to do a little running. They can carry or push/pull bigger things along with them and also "drive" themselves around on little cars. They love to climb up and down things like stairs and furniture, climbing toys, and your lap! They can steadily squat to look at things, stretch up high to reach at things, push, pull and throw all sorts of things, and are expert at knocking things down. With the amount of movement and exploration happening, falling down is a big part of learning at this stage.

24 MONTHS:
A two year old has got the basics of moving down. They can walk forwards and backwards and run fairly well, can start and stop quickly, and stairs are nothing (except a heart attack for mom). They have more balance and now avoid more obstacles than they crash into (yay!). They dance and hop around, and can climb up, over and through many things with ease. They have the coordination to throw under and overhand, and chase and kick a ball.

HOME LIFE:
First they're pulling themselves to standing by holding onto the couch and coffee table, next thing you know they're climbing up and leaping off of them (especially if they have sibs). They start the year by rolling a ball to you and end by nailing you in the head with a rock from 2 feet away. And while their first steps were so exciting, you soon spend at least half your time chasing them. They also may freak out or try to run away almost every time you change their diaper or clothes (serious gross motor skill action!). You will not be allowed to sit down at restaurants, or anywhere else, for that matter. Toddlers are not big fans of sitting still (unless they're not feeling well). They prefer climbing up to high dangerous places, dashing towards perilous streets, and looking for sharp objects to wave around and things to pull down onto themselves. Good times!

HELPFUL HINTS:
Give your child every opportunity to move those muscles and get that energy out. It can be hard to leave the house, but do it! Go for walks around the neighborhood, even if it takes an hour to go around one block - that's an amazing adventure for them. Parks with grassy slopes and playing fields are great outdoor places to let them practice walking, running, and falling down safely They'll love going on the playground equipment too. You can find a favorite stairway and go visit it often to let them go up and down, holding their hand or staying right behind them. This seems to be a skill they need to practice a lot. I also like nature trails. It's good to invest in a good baby carrier, they can come in really handy on long outings. Toddlers tire easily and are very slow. Also, always bring (healthy) food along - they cry less when they have something in their mouth!

UTILIZE ACTIVITIES:
Walk to a friend's house and do an activity with them. Or bring a smaller activity on an outing and do it at the park when your toddler needs some down time or you want to sit. When you can't get out, turn on some music and try the Jingle Bracelet (page 102) or Maraca (page 100) activities and get your groove on!

FINE MOTOR SKILLS

Fine motor movements are actions that involve the movement of the smaller muscles of the body, mainly in the fingers, toes, wrists, lips, and tongue. Fine motor skills require the development of hand eye coordination, the strengthening of the muscles involved and the ability to coordinate those muscles in order to perform the actions a person wants to do.

Fine motor abilities in children start with things such as picking up small objects and holding a spoon and advance to holding small items, eating, turning pages, then buttoning clothing, cutting with scissors, writing, and using phones and keyboards, for example. *ref2

12 MONTHS:
At 12 months babies can grasp very small objects between their thumb and first fingers and find their mouth pretty well, so they can feed themselves small and soft foods. They can also hold their own bottle or sippy and drink from it. Play skills include exploring textures with their hands, passing things from one hand to another, placing items in containers then taking or dumping them out, knocking two items together, and purposefully releasing (dropping) things. When it's time to get dressed, they may "help" by holding out an arm or a leg.

18 MONTHS:
With their improved hand eye coordination toddlers can hold both a cup and spoon and enjoy using them, with some spilling. They can stack a few blocks or stacking toys at a time, and grasp and play around with knobbed puzzles. They are also able use both hands together to hold something in front of them. They can use the pointer finger and can point to familiar objects in books, and turn the pages of a board book. If given a crayon or marker they will scribble spontaneously. They can take off shoes and socks and sometimes more, and also place a hat or other object on their head.

24 MONTHS:
Kids now have a vastly more developed ability to use their fingers and hands. They mouth things less now as instead their hands manipulate objects with greater ease and skill. They can do more focused activities with much smaller objects, like placing rings on sticks, pegs on a pegboard, and bead stringing. Stacks and block towers grow taller, to four blocks or more. Given a paintbrush, this age group can paint with whole arm movements and when scribbling try to imitate a circle or line. They can do simple chopping with soft foods (and dull knives!), and begin to help dressing themselves.

HOME LIFE:
Warning: Nothing is off limits to these kids if it's in their reach.Toddlers are just driven to touch things. They will grab anything that interests them and bang it, smash it, or drop, sweep or throw it to the floor (after tasting it!). They especially love to do this to large piles of folded laundry, and older siblings' precious lego creations. Any important paper in their reach they will rip up, chew up, or scribble all over (or all three).This goes for books and walls too. Actually, just always keep pens out of their reach!" They often like to feed themselves, which of course is messy. They keep on putting things in their

mouth the entire year.

HELPFUL HINTS:
Let them eat on their own if they want to,and use your dog for a vacuum cleaner. Read board books together. Let them explore your belongings under supervision- but do not let them walk away with your keys. Ever. Let them dig in the dirt and sand and play in water with hands and spoons and shovels and buckets, and go hunting for rocks and flowers and leaves and seeds. Let them have as many sensory experiences with their hands that you can both at home and when you are out. Have toys and activities on hand that involve fine motor manipulation, and encourage their use.

UTILIZE ACTIVITIES:
The activities in this book are both fun and excellent for fine motor skills practice, and when you put things that interest them in their hands, they're not touching other things! Do these activities with your child as often as you can get them interested. Keep a few on hand or out all the time, rotating, to give your child lots of opportunities for sensory play and fine motor practice - they need a ton of it.

COMMUNICATION

Communication is the ability to clearly and effectively convey and receive messages to and from others both verbally and through body language, including facial expressions, eye contact, arm movement, and posture. *ref3

12 MONTHS:
At one, babies really enjoy babbling away in their own secret language as they practice making sounds, and are forming their very first words, like "dada" and "mama"! They listen and watch closely and try to copy the sounds and actions you make. They might shake their head for "no" and use short exclamations, like "uh-oh!" They start showing an understanding of things you say and respond, like looking when they hear their name, raising arms when you ask "up?," and altering behavior when told "no."

18 MONTHS:
Toddlers now understand much more of what you say and respond to it. Their vocabulary has grown by leaps and bounds, though they can't verbalize it all just yet. While they can say a few to a few dozen clear words, they probably understand close to 10 times more! They experiment with sounds all the time, babbling, singing, and making funny noises with their lips and tongues. With limited words they learn to add tone, inflection and gestures to help get their meaning across. A common way they draw attention to things that interest them is by pointing or leading you by the hand.

24 MONTHS:
By 2 years, kids have a vocabulary of fifty to hundreds of words and gain new ones each day, copying sounds more easily now. Some chatter will still be hard to understand, though pronunciation is clearer and the sounds of vowels and more consonants are improving. They easily form 2-4 word phrases and add meaning through facial expressions and body language.They love to ask and answer questions and be included in conversation. Despite the larger vocabulary, "me, mine, hey" and "no" may be the most used words.

HOME LIFE:
Kids may be learning how to talk this year, but crying still seems to be their fave way of saying something. (Or shouting, or whining, or other horrible noises coming from their face!). When you know what you want but you can't say it, it's frustrating! When they do talk though, it's so fun and amazing. There is nothing more adorable than their little voices saying "mom!", " 'poon"

or…. "marshmallow!" They are also super cuddly and affectionate (yes, this is communication!). My favorite is when they lead you around by the hand - even when you don't want to go, how can you resist? I also love it when they place your hand on things and look at you plaintively, as if you should know what they want! At some point near the end of this year you will realize by the way they respond to you that they seem to understand almost every single thing you say.

HELPFUL HINTS:
Talk to your child (when you feel like it), in a natural way, starting when they are very young about what's going on with and around them. When they start to talk, repeat what they say, expanding their words or short phrases into sentences. Be encouraging, expressive, and make eye contact while talking when possible. Look for opportunities to repeat things throughout the day, like numbers and colors. Read out loud to them and help them point out their favorite objects and name them. Sing!

UTILIZING ACTIVITIES:
Any of the activities are excellent opportunities for verbalizing with your child. Casually mention the colors and numbers of the objects they are using (here's the red stick!). It's the perfect opportunity to use adjectives like soft, hard, puffy, heavy, light, loud, inside, outside, and so on. The learning process is accelerated and the words have deeper meaning to the child when they are also experiencing them sensorily.

COGNITIVE

Cognition refers to conscious mental activities, and includes thinking, reasoning, understanding, learning, and remembering. Cognitive skill development in children is the progressive building of these learning skills, and the ability to apply them. *ref4

12 MONTHS:
At this age, babies transition from more passive observation to interaction and basic problem solving as they gain the power to explore objects around them more closely. They do this in various ways, like shaking, banging, dropping and throwing. They look for and find hidden and dropped objects fairly easily, and look for objects in a room or in books when asked. They show understanding of the uses of everyday objects, like cups, brushes and phones. They achieve simple goals, like crawling to something attractive and picking it up, or moving something to a new spot.

18 MONTHS:
These toddlers know what is "theirs," and where things belong, and can help look for things to bring to you or put away. They really love to manipulate and affect their environment - opening and closing doors, drawers and boxes, turning knobs, flipping light switches, turning on the tap and flooding your bathroom! They will look for and point out objects in familiar places or favorite books.They know a few body parts by now, the names and sounds of favorite animals, and names of familiar people and places. They start to play simple pretend, like feeding a stuffed animal or doll. Perhaps most exciting of all, they can follow simple directions and requests (when they feel like it!).

24 MONTHS:
Two year olds can use their new speaking skills to express their needs and desires. They can respond to questions directed at them and also to two-step instructions ("go get your jacket and hang it up"). They'll also ask lots of questions of their own and begin to grasp concepts like quantity (more, gone, etc.) and space (up, down, out, etc.), and can find cleverly hidden objects.

They can now do more complex things, like sort and match by shape and color, complete simple puzzles and do two things at once, like sing and perform movements for "action songs." And imagination flows as make-believe play grows.

HOME LIFE:
Everything is new, interesting, and needs to be explored. Toddlers are capable of doing (or trying to do) many things now, but they're not "trained" yet! They don't stop when you say stop, and they don't come when you call! They destroy and fall off of many things. The best you can do is try to get them, and most of your things, through this year in one piece. Large amounts of your time and attention are required for this. You have to say "No!" and take things away a lot, which seems to anger them, and lead to power struggles, crying (sometimes by both of you), and much bewilderment. It's all part of the process. You find mystery items in your shopping cart, the dog water dumped out every time you fill it, and watch out for your electronics! You never know what they'll get into next, and chances are you will not quite always be able to stay one step ahead..

But ooh, are these guys and girls little charmers! You'll be amazed by how smart they are, and so proud and happy about each new accomplishment. Your heart is melted everyday by their sweetness and lovingness.The first time you realize they're making a joke is awesome. Their excitement about everything is contagious.Sometimes you'd swear they can't get any cuter!

HELPFUL HINTS:
Let your house go a little and try to enjoy this time of wonderment and discovery for your child. Explore nature, visit friends, eat, go shopping, laugh, dance, sing and share sweet moments of cuddles and play. Your baby has become a little buddy and there are many precious moments to be had and much teaching to do. Remember that this time won't last forever. Hug them a lot and write down the cutest things they say and do. As much as you think you'll remember, you won't, so write it down!! Take pictures and video. Also, it helps if you put anything breakable up high, and don't try to make too many plans .Count to ten when you need to - remember, these kids aren't trying to be bad, they're just trying to figure things out. Try to find a good babysitter for those times you need a break. It's essential.

UTILIZE ACTIVITIES:
Activities are amazing for helping your little one stay busy and learning through exploration. By their very nature they are perfect for cognitive growth as they involve use of various senses and skill sets. Use them at home or on the go, as you will need to occupy and redirect your toddler frequently.

SOCIAL / EMOTIONAL

Social-emotional development includes a child's experience, expression, and management of emotions and the ability to establish positive and rewarding relationships with others. *ref5

12 MONTHS:
At this stage babies are becoming more aware of the people around them and their emotions. They smile when smiled at, or may get distressed when someone around them is sad or upset. They cuddle with and show affection to familiar people. They love to share eye contact and smiles and giggles. They are still very connected to parents and caregivers and likely show fear and anxiety when separated from them.

18 MONTHS:
Toddlers begin to show more independence and will explore alone, but still want a parent nearby to touch base with frequently. They are curious about other kids, but not ready to play with them just yet. They often play alongside other kids instead, and may compete for toys or attention or not always relate peacefully. They still relate highly to adults though, and may hand you toys or lead you in play with them. They are goal oriented and eager to try new things, and this can lead to frustration and temper tantrums at times when things don't work out as they'd hoped. But this is also a time when toddlers begin to show care and affection for others, and can start to learn cooperation and self-control. Fear of strangers and separation anxiety are still high.

24 MONTHS:
Independence continues to grow and they continue to imitate the behavior of adults and older children around them. They finally start to get excited about playing with others and and now you will see the emergence of defiant behavior (doing what they've been told not to do). They are aware of themselves as separate from others and know their likes and dislikes based on their experiences. They spend more and more time away from their caregiver but still love and need lots of closeness and affection and will seek it constantly throughout the day. Personality and sense of humor really shine through. Separation anxiety finally begins to calm.

HOME LIFE:
These kids show a lot of independence by the end of the year, but they still want to be held a lot. They just need it! They love camaraderie and connection and being part of family activities and doing what everybody else does. They really watch and mimic parents and siblings in adorable tiny people ways. They can get pretty frustrated or angry when you don't let them participate in the ways they want to (ie - handling your crystal goblets, driving your car), and sometimes try things like hitting. They can be great little helpers at this age though, when you give them things they can do. They're not exactly looking for friends just yet, but will have fun playing with other young kids that they spend a lot of time with.

HELPFUL HINTS:
This is an extremely pivotal time for brain development in kids, and loving one-on-one relationships are actually an essential need for the healthiest brain development. Be loving, encouraging, and connected to your child. Be responsive to their needs, not just physical, but emotional. When they try to tell you something, stop and listen, and help them solve their problem or figure it out. Include them in the activities of the home, and give them a strong base from which to venture out and try things in the world. Remember that they are little sponges right now, so model good behavior when you can, as how you behave now is how they will behave later (a great motivator for

having patience and controlling yourself!). Model joy and fun too, be silly with your kids, dance and sing around the house (at least once in awhile!), and make time for the good things in life, like quality time with family and friends.

UTILIZE ACTIVITIES:
Activities are great ways to pass the time with family and friends while naturally strengthening bonds and growing social skills. Shared fun creates a connection that little ones really enjoy. They are also a great way to engage a child and and connect when they feel overwhelmed. Do an activity with them when they seem overwhelmed or insecure. The familiarity and routine of it will be soothing to their brain.

ALL ABOUT ACTIVITIES

- Activities are an awesome way for your child to learn through play, while practicing all of their basic skills.

- Activities involve many types of play: _Challenging_ play that gets children experimenting and problem solving, and helps them develop concentration, creativity, and confidence, _Sensory_ play that helps them add information to their brain about the world around them, and _Active_ play that helps develop their coordination and motor skills.

- The variety of materials and colors used in activities creates a rich environment for little ones learning through their senses, making your home more enjoyable for them, and you.

- Activities often involve the use of many senses plus movement, all of which has a deeper and more complex impact on the brain during the learning process.

- They offer natural opportunities for vocabulary and social developments.

- They involve repetitive movements, which help strengthen kids' bodies and refine their motor skills more quickly. This helps develop muscle memory, where the basic actions are practiced enough to become almost automatic, allowing kids to move onto more complicated actions sooner.

- They help children develop concentration and the ability to focus on tasks for increasing periods of time - growing their attention spans. The ability to focus and complete tasks are two of the most important qualities needed for success in life, along with social skills and creativity.

Concentration is learned and nurtured through practice, and activities can help your child develop and lay down strong brain pathways in this area that will benefit them life long. There are many amazing resources online and in books about this topic, and I encourage everyone to learn more about early childhood brain development, for your benefit and your child's.

OPEN ENDED PLAY

Activities also nourish creativity, and can provide a starting point for **open ended play**. Open ended play is playing with objects that have multiple uses and endless possibilities, *ref6 like blocks, balls, boxes, fabrics, paints, clay, pompoms, pipe cleaners and so on. This type of play is best for growing kids because it fosters creativity and brain growth in every area of development.

Activities give a structural base to get started with this kind of play. Structure actually stimulates imagination. Suppose you had never seen a ball or a ballcourt and someone just left you at a court with only the ball and your imagination. You could come up with a few ideas, but if they also showed you how to play several games first, you could not only play those games, but you'd also be able to build on those ideas by coming up with many variations of each one. One idea leads to another!

Activities are like that, not only for the children doing them, but for the adults who provide them.

They are the perfect way to help cultivate creativity, not only in your child, but in yourself!

Many activities can be used as a starting points for playing with open ended play items, and that's why they help develop creativity and the ability to play independently. An activity can be intended for practicing certain skills, but can also be enjoyed many other ways. (Bonus: This is much less boring for the parent!)

I (Heather) found my own creative outlet within the structure of these simple activities as well, finally getting down craft materials I had stored for years and putting them to use, much to all of my children's delight! And that's just the beginning.

WHEN CAN YOU DO ACTIVITIES?

Some people are more scheduled and will want to set a regular time that will be a special time to look forward to. It could be once a day, once a week or once a month. It could be just you and your toddler, or you can make it a family time.

But once you've learned a few activities that your child likes there are no limits. You can pull them out at anytime you want to spend some quality time with or need to occupy your toddler.

Some times that activities might be helpful to you:

- When you want to talk on the phone or skype

- When traveling or in the car (with safety in mind)

- While shopping

- When your other kids need your help with homework or need attention

- When you need to make dinner and can't get them off your leg

- At a restaurant or coffee shop (if you haven't given up on those yet!)

- When you want to have an adult conversation

- When you need a quick distraction

- When you're stuck inside on a rainy day

- When you have to wait somewhere with your child

Many of these moments can be frustrating with a toddler - phone call or conversation, anyone? But if you can get them engaged enough in a quiet activity, it can make things go more smoothly and pleasantly for everyone when you just have to get things done.

Activities are not bound to the home! Because many of them are small and contained, they're great for on the go. And because they're homemade and inexpensive, you don't have to get super stressed about losing them anywhere.

You don't even need to have the whole activity with you. Just stick a long ribbon in your pocket for your child to pull on, or carry some craft sticks for them to push through an empty coffee cup lid in a pinch. Or improvise with materials you find while you are out. Once you and your toddler are trained in the art of activities, you'll be more creative everywhere!

THE BEST GRAB & GO ACTIVITIES!

Activities are great for socializing too. One of the best parts of this whole project has been getting to hang out with Nicolette while the kids were happily busy with their activities!

You can have fun doing these activities at home alone with your toddler, but why not invite another mom friend over to visit while her little one shares in the fun, or take the activities along to the park or a friend's house? It'll be more fun for all, you're sure to impress, and you just may be able to hold a conversation!

Another idea is a toddler birthday party. These activities would be great for keeping a bunch of toddlers entertained and busy, and and many would make fantastic party gifts for the guests to take home!

They also make great gifts for friends who are traveling with small children, or your own kids if you're traveling. Your friend will be grateful for the diversion and won't have to worry if the "toys" get lost.

GETTING STARTED AND DOING THE ACTIVITIES

Just get started! Choose an activity and do it!

Remember that when you spend quality time doing activities like these with your toddler, you're laying the groundwork for a child who is calmer, more self led and creative. Taking the time to give your children 10- 20 minutes of concentrated attention when they need it throughout the day satisfies their need for attention, closeness and security and allows them to relax and play independently for longer periods. Try it.

Don't worry about being perfect. Even if every activity you do looks like a Pinterest fail, who cares? Certainly not your toddler, who just wants to spend time with you and see your smiling face. Luckily one-year-olds are not harsh critics, unless maybe it's about your cooking! (Besides, you will learn from each "mistake" and get better - the only way is by doing!)

Keep adding new activities to your repertoire. The more you have on hand, and the more of them you know, the easier and quicker they are to go to when you need them.

Even if it takes you a month to do one activity, at least you've done one. If you need to buy a glue gun one week, felt the next, lentils the next, and make the bean bags the next, great! At least you're progressing! And if it was that hard for you, you're going to feel pretty cool when you finally get it done. (But in the meantime I hope you did at least one simpler one!)

Remember that you are not just training your toddler, you're training yourself, stretching and growing your own creativity and reviving your sense of fun.

The more you do activities, the better you will be at it as your child gets older and it gets more interesting!

Go with the flow when it comes to your child's abilities and how he does the activities. Remember that toddlers need to explore, have lots of energy, and may not "get" doing activities right away. Also, their average attention span is only a few minutes. Be realistic in your expectations of your child, and remember, process over product! Just have fun, no matter how it goes!

Be Patient!! No matter how cool your activity, your toddler will still be a toddler, crying, getting frustrated, throwing or ripping up your materials at times, or not be interested at all. They'll be happy one minute, freaking out the next. Content one minute, needing you the next. Activities are not happy pills that make any of that go away! But over the course of this year, toddlers will learn to be more controlled and calm, and spending time patiently with them on things like activities will help speed that process.

Be social! Toddlers love playing alongside other kids. It also inspires creativity in them and is so much more fun. It's also good for you. Having another adult to talk to this year can be crucial, since having small kids can be very isolating. It can be hard to get out of the house, but make an effort for your own sake and reach out to another mom - believe me, she can relate.

If you are a very organized person with some space, start a small playgroup doing these activities on a weekly basis! (Or do it at a park.) Don't insist that anyone wash their hair or bring any food to share, especially if they have multiple kids.

Combine some of these activities or do more than one in a sitting for longer play. Keep less messy activities out and your toddler may run out to play and then come back to them repeatedly. Toddlers can be interested in many things at once and have a lot of energy to burn.

Part of doing activities is to help encourage and develop parallel and independent play. If your child is enjoying the activity on their own and you are able to do something else nearby, go for it. (Then try not to get frustrated when they cry and call you back. Baby steps!)

Extend play by (1) Being very involved and paying attention to your child, or (2) Introducing new elements or ideas whenever your child's interest starts to wane. (When your child tires of putting the pompoms in the tube, for example, start tossing them into a nearby basket instead). You can do this for quite some time when you really want to spend time with your child or have a lot of time to kill. Open ended play!

Watch for motions that they really enjoy (for my child it is the pouring activity from one cup to another), and help them practice those skills during free play by giving them what they need (in our case, cups). They will get much more engaged in their play and play longer!

Consider decluttering your house by moving unused toys out and having activities available in their place. (To me, activities are our new toys.) If you think your child is watching too much media, start to cut back by giving them brain building activities to occupy their time instead.

Involve your older kids as much as possible. They love activities and your attention too! Also, older kids are great for doing the activities with your little ones, and it promotes sibling bonding and can give you some relief.

If your husband acts like he doesn't know what to do with your toddler or your other kids, activities are the perfect place to start. Children can be boring and mystifying to play with, and activities give a focal point for both the child and the adult - that can even stretch and evolve into more creative play!

Above all, have fun, and decide to make quality time with your kids a priority.. This is a gentle reminder (to myself as well) that loving attention is a need. Even a few minutes a day with each one will make a huge difference to them (and you!).

Kids are amazingly insecure and need to know they are loved and cherished as much as they need food. Inviting them into a short activity with you will allow the space for you to sit together and connect and converse - and let your child know they are important to you. Yes, activities have brain benefits and are fun, but they can also be a tool you can use for yourself - to help you stop the busyness for a minute and enjoy life with your precious loved ones! I hope that you do!

HOW TO USE THE ACTIVITIES IN THIS BOOK

This book is intended to be used as and when you need it. Most of the ideas in this book are simple yet engaging.

1 year olds are more interested in the process than the outcome.

Don't be discouraged if your child does something totally different from what the activity was intended to do. The same goes for the child not being able to complete the activity. Put it aside and try again in a few weeks.

The activities are mostly from household items and easy to source materials, such as pom poms.

We provide helpful tips as often as we can and hope you find these useful while doing the activity with your child.

Most of these activities are not just for 1 year olds and if you have older children you will often find that they too will join in the activity and explore the ideas.

You will also often see notes with the authors' names when a specific voice is used such as the example below:

Nicolette: I started using my kitchen serving trays with the kids after fights broke out about whose pom pom or bead it was that was on the table. The trays helped keep things all in one place and define the space that was solely for the child using it.

You will also notice that Heather has more detailed comments on all the activities as her 1 year old son Harvey was the star of the show!

Provided below all the activities is a space to write your own notes on how your child did with the activity. These help you remember what happened last time so that you have an even better time this time around.

"Love and exploration are as important as food"

- Deborah Mcnelis, The Brain Development Series

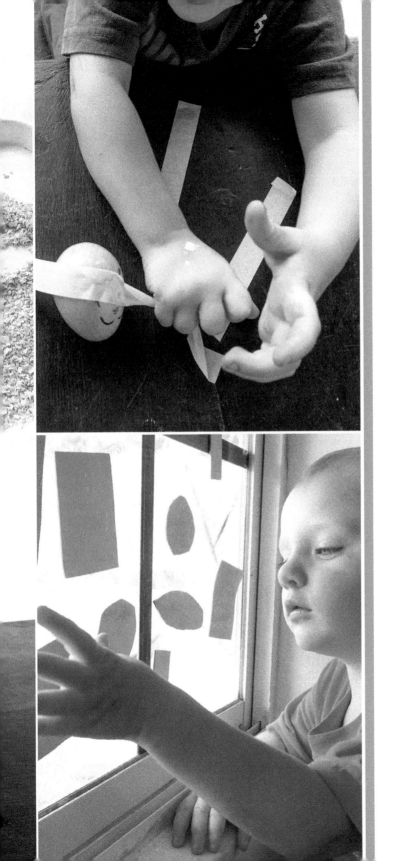

ACTIVITIES

WATER SCOOPING & POURING

Materials:
- Sensory bin / table
- Cups
- Jug

Directions:
Set up your sensory bin and add in an inch or two of water. Demonstrate to your child the action of scooping then pouring from one cup to the other.

One of the things children of this age struggle with is staying over the tub so encourage this if you see it.

Heather:
Doing this activity just once seemed to awaken an awareness in Harvey of the joys of scooping and pouring. Now, whenever he's near water, he does it, usually totally independently and absorbed.

If you do this activity indoors with a tub, it's a good opportunity to guide them in keeping the water in and over the tub to help them develop self-control and memory (and keep things dry!).

Bonus:
A few days after we did this activity, Harvey pulled a chair up to the sink while I did dishes and copied the pouring activity. The floor got washed a little, but it was worth it having my little one by my side. It was a sweet moment that probably wouldn't have happened before we did the activity.

Tips/Variations:
- Do this activity outside or on a tiled floor. Place a towel down to soak up excess water.
- Don't give them too many cups, they only have two hands!
- Make sure you have enough cups on hand for siblings who want to join in.
- Observe which hands they favor and if they are going back and forth with both.

Bigger Kids/As They Grow:
- Use one large and one small container/cup. Count how many small fill the large, and then pour back into the smaller cup.
- Have them carry water to another container or to water a flower in the yard. This adds gross motor skills and keeps them happily busy.

Your Notes:

_____

_____

_____

_____

_____

DUPLO MOVING IN WATER

Materials:
- Sensory bin / table
- Duplo train or cars basically anything with wheels

Directions:
Set up your sensory bin with about an inch of water and add your vehicles. Adding duplo vehicles to the water brings on a whole new aspect of play with toys that kids could otherwise be bored with.

Heather:
Harvey had more fun using the cars to splash water than anything else, but that's OK. I love using a clear bin as it's brighter, inside and out.

Bonus:
To do this at home, I moved some Duplos from a clear bin into a cardboard box so we could use the bin. My eldest (8) came out and played parallel to us the whole time and has been playing with the legos and box for weeks.

So, doing this for my one year old stoked my eldest's creativity, and I get to enjoy watching it. It's so true that when you change things up even a little, kids notice things all over again!

Tips/Variations:
- Put a swimsuit on your little one so you don't worry about wet clothes.
- Towels are a definite necessity.
- Use clear bins with water activities when possible.

Bigger Kids/As They Grow:
- Just let them have fun with it. You don't have to do much for kids that have water and lego!

Your Notes:

_____

_____

_____

_____

_____

OBJECT SCOOPING

Materials:
- Sensory Bin / Table
- Objects that float such as duplo blocks, plastic easter eggs, plastic balls
- Scoop such as one from the sandbox or a plain kitchen sieve / strainer

Directions:
Add 2-4 inches of water to your sensory bin and add in your items. Demonstrate to your child the action of using the scoop to catch the floating objects.

Heather:
Harvey was more into picking up the objects and putting them into the sieve by hand while another child held it. Then he wanted me to do the motions. He was taking it in more than anything as we'd really never practiced this skill, so I look forward to doing this one more and watching him improve.

Bonus:
An hour after we did the activity, he took the sieve off the table and started filling it with toys from a bucket and then dumping them back in, and did that for quite some time, standing between my legs while I got to sit and talk to Nicolette for awhile. Works for me!

Tips/Variations:
- Allow your child to explore different ways to play with the sieve.
- You can also use objects that float, and natural materials like stones and leaves.

Bigger Kids/As They Grow:
- You can incorporate counting and patterns - trying to scoop a certain number of objects each time or increasing the number of objects with each scoop.
- You can incorporate colors by only using or scooping up certain color objects.
- Have some objects that sink and others that float and try to scoop out sunken objects without getting the floating ones on the way up. You can also throw in some science with this one!

Your Notes:
_____

_____

_____

_____

_____

PAINTING WITH WATER

Materials:
- Large paint brushes
- A small amount of water in a bowl
- Chalk board or sidewalk

Directions:
This activity has so many possibilities. Paint with water on a chalkboard or on your sidewalk.

Make faces, paint flowers or simply make spots!

Heather:
I loved this one - it was so effortless and fun for the moms! Harvey babbled and worked away happily alongside Nicolette's kids who all came running for their own paintbrush.

The kids were totally uninhibited, no one worried about "messing up," like they might if they were working on paper. We hung out and talked while the kids hit it, and got to enjoy seeing the individual creativity of each child - and the only cleanup was a couple of swipes with a towel to clean up dripped water.

Bonus:
The movements involved are awesome for building fine and complex gross motor skills and balance at the same time.

Tips/Variations:
- Use a big enough brush so the kids can see their brushstrokes.

Bigger Kids/As They Grow:
- Draw or show them a shape and let them practice it.
- Have them do alphabet letters or their name or numbers. Doing the motion with the whole arm is great for helping them learn the right way to draw a letter.
- Let them paint their masterpiece and admire it!

Your Notes:

_____

_____

_____

_____

_____

RAIN NOISE

Materials:
- Aluminum foil cooking tray
- Bottle with a shaker lid, or with holes poked in the lid
- Blue food coloring

Directions:
Fill your bottle with water and add a drop of food coloring. Place the cooking tray in a bin to contain the water mess or do this activity outside. Let the water pour out through the many small holes of your bottle to make a rain noise on the cooking tray.

Once the water is all out of the containers you can extend this activity by adding another tray so that water is scooped from one tray to the other and back again.

Heather:
When this one is done outside on the grass, it's nearly effortless. Harvey was absolutely mesmerized. Nicolette had an entire gallon of colored water so for a while I refilled the bottles for him.

Once all the water was out, we took the lids off and he scooped and poured, his favorite activity. The light blue color of the water was lovely and calming. The activity is fascinating and fun for a toddler and naturally extends in ways that will keep them playing for a while.

Bonus:
At first Harvey wanted me to share in his joy, and refill his bottles, but when we transitioned to the scooping and pouring, he didn't need me and became so absorbed I was able to slip away and give some attention to my 4 year old, which was a huge blessing in that moment. He didn't even notice I'd gone up to the porch for about 10 minutes!

Tips/Variations:
- Don't overdo the coloring, keep it light.
- Give them a few different colors.
- Demonstrate pouring the water from different levels and draw their attention to the sounds that it makes.

Bigger Kids/As They Grow:
- Use primary colors and have fun blending them.
- Add a spoon, baster or dropper for more fine motor practice fun.

Your Notes:

_____

_____

_____

_____

_____

WINDOW STICKING

Materials:
- Foam Shapes
- Dish with very shallow water
- A window

Directions:
Place your foam shapes in a bit of water to make them wet. Show your child how the wet foam sticks on the window surface.

Depending on what foam shapes you have make pictures with your child's help!

Heather:
Harvey caught on quickly and enjoyed sticking the shapes to the window, but looking outside made him want to go outside and play! (Nicolette does have a great yard.) It's a creative activity that requires some focus on Harvey's part and attention from me, so a quieter time would work better for my child with this one.

Bonus:
One day, I did the Duplo in the Water activity with Harvey (and, of course the other kids) and when I emptied the water, instead of drying the inside I threw some hand cut foam shapes, store bought foam cutouts (hearts, stars, animal and plant shapes) and foam letters into the box and my 4 and 6 year olds played with them for over 30 minutes, while Harvey went off and played something else.

I doubled the activities and the playtime with almost no effort, and had some precious moments with my older kids.

Tips/Variations:
- Let your toddler stick these to the fridge while you're working in the kitchen.
- Practice color and shape vocabulary as you play.

Bigger Kids/As They Grow:
- Make animals, structures or scenes with the shapes and cutouts.
- Make rows, patterns or designs.
- Do holiday or seasonal themed windows.
- Let kids use foam letters to spell out their names or other simple words.
- Let kids test different surfaces (best to supervise) to see where the foam will stick and where it won't.

Your Notes:

_____

_____

_____

_____

POM POMS IN A TUBE

Materials:

- Pom poms
- Tube or toilet roll

Directions:

Provide a handful of pom poms for your child to post in the tube. This activity is great for things disappearing then reappearing on the other end. (Concept of "Object Permanence")

Heather:
We had fun with this for ten minutes or so. Typical for my child, he enjoyed dumping the pom poms out more than putting them in. Sometimes he wanted me to put the poms in the tube or hold the tube for him. This one is great for concentration and fine motor, especially with the narrower tube, and best done when your child is not feeling energetic!

Bonus:
At home, my 3 year old really enjoyed doing this alongside Harvey with a couple of toilet paper tubes on the coffee table. It gave him a sense of accomplishment and kept Harvey interested longer, while I worked in the kitchen. Only put out as many poms as you want to clean up off the floor!

Tips/Variations:
- Challenge their fine motor skills by using a smaller diameter tube when it seems too easy.
- Plug the bottom of the tube and have them fill it up, then let them fall out the bottom.
- Experiment to see how many poms they can get through the opening at once.
- Try letting older kids play this with toddlers when they need occupying.

Bigger Kids/As They Grow:
- Say the color of the poms as you put them in.
- Count the poms as you put them in.
- Tape the tubes to a table and sort by color. (You could color the tubes first, or if you're feeling extra awesome and have time, glue the right color pom to it.)
- Set a few tubes on the table and put some pompoms in only one. Then, mix up the tubes. Can they guess which one has the poms? Kids will also love to be the mixer upper and have you be the guesser.
- The same as just above, but put a different color pom in each tube.

Your Notes:

_____

_____

_____

_____

_____

PIPE CLEANERS & HOLES

Materials:

- Pipe cleaners
- Strainer with large enough holes or anything else like a small basket with holes

Directions:

Fold over the ends of the pipe cleaners to prevent your child accidently poking themselves with the inner wire of the pipe cleaner. Demonstrate the activity with lots of encouragement and soon your child will be trying it for themselves!

If your child has trouble with the lengths of the pipe cleaners another idea is to either fold them in half making it shorter but also thicker or to actually cut the pipe cleaners in half. A wire cutter is the best tool for the job.

Heather:
This is an activity that requires focus and concentration for a one year old, best done when they're already in a quiet mood. It's great for fine motor skills, and for working on together.

My active child has a hard time slowing down for activities like this because we've never done them, but the other kids' enthusiasm got him interested for 5 minutes or so.

Bonus:
One night when I was trying to make dinner and Harvey was fussy I thought of this activity. I grabbed the colander from the cabinet, some pipe cleaners from the shelf and voila! My 6 and 4 year olds ran over because I never get out the pipe cleaners and they love them and they helped keep Harvey occupied while I cooked.

Tips/Variations:
- You may have to stay near and encourage your child until they get more used to this one.
- Try sneaking small plastic or stuffed animals or other fun objects under the colander.
- Turn the colander both ways so kids can put them in from both sides.
- Have them both push and pull the pipe cleaners through.

Bigger Kids/As They Grow:
- Use only pipecleaners of one color to work on color recognition.
- Do areas in different colors or in designs or patterns.
- Have your child weave the pipe cleaners in and out through the holes.
- First thread large beads or round cereal on the pipe cleaner, then watch them fly off as you pull it through the hole.

Your Notes:

_____

_____

_____

_____

_____

POSTING STICKS CONTAINER

Materials:

- Cylindrical container with a lid, example a pringles can
- Jumbo craft sticks
- Colorful tape (optional)

Directions:

Clean out your container and cover it with wrapping paper or colorful tape. Cut a hole on the top rectangular in shape and large enough to post the craft sticks through.

Demonstrate the activity to the child.

Did you know that this container can make a noise once it has sticks in it?

Heather:
Harvey loved putting just one stick in, then taking off the lid to see it and take/dump it back out. He got extra fine motor exercise in by taking the lid on and off, but needed my help with that, so I needed to stay with him.

He also grabbed other nearby objects to see if they would fit through the hole, and liked shaking it to hear the noise and looking inside for the stick(s) when he pulled off the lid. Great lessons in object permanence.

Bonus:
This is very easily transportable activity that doubles as a noisemaker.

Tips/Variations:
- Help your toddler explore all the ways to make noises with these materials.
- After using the sticks, let them experiment with trying to put other objects through the slot, it's a great opportunity for exploring space and size and exposing them to vocabulary.

Bigger Kids/As They Grow:
- Count the sticks and/or say the color of each one as it's put in the slot.
- From a pile of sticks have them put in only one color.
- From a pile of sticks have them put in a certain amount of each color.

Your Notes:

_____

_____

_____

_____

COLOR INSIDE A BOX

Materials:

- A box large enough to fit your child
- Wax crayons

Directions:

Place the box on the floor and place your child inside the box. The flaps of the box should be open.

Show your child how you draw on the inside of the box encouraging them to copy you. Sit back and watch the magic happen.

Heather:
Most fun for Harvey was having us all gathered around the box and coloring with him. I'd tried to get him to do this on his own before, but it didn't work. This time he really felt like the center of attention, and it was fun for all of us. He pulled my hand in to color with him, and then colored where I did.

When he lost interest in the coloring we still played quite a bit longer, just tickling and laughing. He laid down on his back and just looked at the drawings and up at us and the ceiling.

Bonus:
Your kid gets the fun and fine motor exercise of coloring while safely contained.

Tips/Variations:
- Do hidden or partially hidden pictures under the bottom flaps and then pull the flaps back to look at them.
- A squarish box is nice as all sides are easily accessible.
- Let your older kids help and/or participate, it's more fun.
- You can also let kids sticker the inside of the box.

Bigger Kids/As They Grow:
- Draw a circle or shape and have them scribble inside of it.
- Draw a circle or shape and have them try to copy it.
- Play tic tac toe.
- Ask them to stick a body part out and tickle it.
- Trace their feet and hands for them.

Your Notes:

_____

_____

_____

_____

POM POMS IN A BOX

Materials:
- A large box big enough to fit your child
- A bag of pom poms
- Optional items to hide in the pom poms

Directions:
Place the box on the floor with the flaps open. Place your child in the box and empty the bag of pom poms in with them. Watch them kick their feet and roll around the pom poms!

Nicolette:
A bonus idea to do with this same box is to put something else in it like plastic animals and play find the hidden objects.

Heather:
This was one of our very favorite activities. So fun. Harvey soaked up the attention as Nicolette and I and her two girls surrounded him, showering poms all over his head (and they mainly stayed in the box!) Nicolette's 2 year old climbed in too and Harvey didn't mind at all.

We had fun putting the poms in their clothes and on their heads. Harvey got obsessed with putting them in his ears! He loved just laying in them and rolling around. We also played tickle. It's an amazing sensory activity, keeps the kids interest a long time, and so easy!

Bonus:
This is such a great way to make a child feel like the center of attention and have a super fun and bonding time - all while you are sitting down!

Tips/Variations:
- You can dangle things and they can try to grab them.
- You can practice body parts by placing pompoms on different body parts and naming them.
- You can practice body parts by asking them to stick a hand, foot, leg or arm, or face out of the box and then grabbing or tickling.
- This makes for great sibling play.
- Hide small objects under the poms for them to search for.
- Get in there with your child once in awhile. It's a great opportunity for cuddling.

Bigger Kids/As They Grow:
- Kids will enjoy this activity as it is for many years.

Your Notes:

_____

_____

_____

_____

_____

CONTACT PAPER STICKING

Materials:
- Contact Paper
- Pom poms
- Construction tape

Directions:
Peel the 2 top corners of your contact paper and place the construction tape in the corners. Tape the contact paper to the wall or fridge. Peel the rest of the backing off and tape the other corners.

Place the pom poms in easy range of the contact paper. Show your child how the pom poms stick to the contact paper.

Heather:
This is an absolute fave. It was funny watching Harvey the first time, because he didn't see the paper and was trying to put the poms on the wall next to it. It's a good challenge and excellent for cognitive skills to understand where the sticky part begins, or why the poms stick certain places and not others.

Bonus:
Harvey was so thrilled with this one, I called my husband that day and asked him to pick up sticky paper on his way home. That night, when Harvey wouldn't go to sleep, instead of getting frustrated I got out the paper and pompoms and not only did we have fun for awhile, but my husband was able to take over! Another night I put a much bigger piece on the wall, and all four of my kids got super involved and creative and we had a nice family time.

Tips/Variations:
- Make sure to tape the corners up before peeling off all the backing.
- Put just a few (10-20) poms in a basket for easier cleanup.
- Try hollow plastic balls, yarn, feathers or big buttons to shake thing up.
- For variation, you can stick the contact paper to the oven door and turn the oven light on.
- Try throwing the pompoms and making them stick.
- Leave the paper on the wall until the stick is gone so they can keep exploring it at their own pace.

Bigger Kids/As They Grow:
- Give them more poms so they can be more creative.
- Suggest animals or plants or themes for them to create (if they need suggestions.)
- Do shapes or letters.
- Test different items to see what will stay and what is too heavy.

Your Notes:

_____

_____

_____

_____

_____

POSTING POM POMS

Materials:
- Container with a lid
- Pom poms

Directions:
Cut 4 holes in the top of the lid large enough to post pom poms through. Replace the lid on the container.

Show your child how the pom poms go into the container and disappear. They will soon join in the fun with you!

Heather:
Harvey liked putting the pompoms in through the holes, but he liked taking off the lid to look inside and then dumping them out even more. He repeated this cycle several times with my help. This will be a good one for me to help work with Harvey on focus and concentration.

Bonus:
When doing the sticky paper pompom activity as a family, Harvey began to get disruptive, so I quickly ran and grabbed an empty old plastic container from the kitchen and poked some holes in it.

He then played another 20 minutes, with some attention from my husband, picking poms up off the floor and putting them through the holes, buying me a little precious extra time and attention for my older kids.

Tips/Variations:
- Throw in some bells for a little extra noise stimulation.
- Take the lid off and try to toss/throw the poms into the container.

Bigger Kids/As They Grow:
- Count the poms as you put them in.
- Sort the poms by color, or ask them to put in or pull out only a certain color.

Your Notes:

_____

_____

_____

_____

_____

STACK & KNOCK BLOCKS

Materials:

- Blocks of various shapes
- Optional plastic animals

Directions:

Place the blocks on the floor and invite your child over to play with them with you. Show your child how you stack the blocks up one by one. Either let them fall over or knock them down. Watching things topple over is great fun.

Use the plastic animals as a new dimension to block stacking. Stack the blocks one or 2 high and balance an animal on the top.

Heather:
It can take awhile to get a one year old to slow down enough to do this, but keep trying as it's great for concentration and fine motor. I like the addition of animals because you can draw out the activity with pretend play and animal sounds.

Don't get frustrated if your child only rolls around in the blocks or keeps knocking your examples over, just roll with it. Kids this age love knocking things down.

Bonus:
Older kids love to get involved and parallel play.

Tips/Variations:
- If your toddler is not interested in stacking the blocks yet, try some silly play with the blocks instead.
- Set up the blocks and let your toddler knock them down. It makes them feel powerful!

Bigger Kids/As They Grow:
- Blocks are open ended and imaginative. Playing blocks with your kids is an easy way to spend quality time with them and have a window into their imagination.

Your Notes:

_____

_____

_____

_____

_____

STRAWS IN A BOTTLE

Materials:

- Spice bottle with largish holes
- Straws

Directions:

Clean out your spice bottle and remove the label. Cut the straws into sizes that fit into the spice bottle.

Spread out the straws and show your child how the straws fit into the spice bottle through the holes.

Heather:
Harvey enjoyed chewing on both the straws and the bottle! Getting him to do this activity required a little bit of coaching from me up front, but then he got into it. He liked putting them in, shaking them out and the noise that they made.

It was also moderately challenging for him at first and he had to concentrate and pay attention to his finger work. Great fine motor practice. He and Nicolette's youngest also had a fun little noise-making shakefest.

Bonus:
I could finally put to use one of those old spice bottles I've been saving! It's a tiny self contained game great for on the go, and you don't have to worry much about losing it. I love taking it out when I go somewhere with the kids and need to keep them calm.

Tips/Variations:
- Use straws in various bright colors and/or stripes.
- Keep one in your bag for when you're out and about and need a distraction for your child.

Bigger Kids/As They Grow:
- Name the colors of the straws as they put them in.
- Count the straws as they put them in.

Your Notes:

_____

_____

_____

_____

_____

STRAWS IN A BOX

Materials:

- Cereal Box
- Straws

Directions:

Use a pen to poke straw size holes in your cereal box. Cut your straw into 3 pieces.

Show your child how the straws fit into the holes in the cereal box.

Heather:

I love this activity for the recycle/reuse aspect, the super simplicity of it, and the fact that the kids can keep playing with the box in many open ended ways. Harvey got really into it.

It's great for fine motor and cognitive skills as he really had to work on his grip, where to hold the straw and how much pressure to put on each hole to get the straw through, plus once he pushed the straws through he looked inside the box for them and had fun pulling and dumping them out.

Bonus:

It's a lot of activity and skills practice for your child for very minimal effort on your part.

Tips/Variations:

- Cut varying lengths of straw.
- Hide or put something unexpected in the box when they're not looking.

Bigger Kids/As They Grow:

- Cut longer pieces that will stand up and then have your child force them through (they will bend easily), or reach in and pull them through the rest of the way.
- Have your child reach into the box and push the straws up through the hole.
- Punch holes in rows, circles or shapes and cut the straws long. Have them fill in the shapes.
- Let kids help you punch the holes or punch them themselves.

Your Notes:

_____

_____

_____

_____

_____

RIBBON PULLING

Materials:

- Large Spice bottle or similar container with a small opening
- Long length of ribbon

Directions:

Clean out your spice bottle. Make one continues length of ribbon as much as will fit in your container and is manageable.

Show your child how the ribbon comes out of the container as they pull it. Then stuff it back in.

Heather:
Harvey really loved pulling the ribbon out and it was fun watching him pull and pull on it, and see the surprised grin on his face as it would keep on coming.

He also liked opening and closing the container. He was not as interested in putting the ribbon back in so I think that would be a good skill to work on with him. It turned into a bit of interactive fun as he liked snapping the lid shut and then saying "open" to me, so it was great for vocab and connecting as well.

Bonus:
The activity can be extended by playing with your child and the ribbon. Ribbons are great for open ended play.

Tips/Variations:
- Make the ribbon as long as you can.
- Have several lengths of ribbons of differing lengths.
- Tie several different colored ribbons together for a long colorful length.

Bigger Kids/As They Grow:
- Use multicolored ribbon and name the colors together.
- Have the kids roll up the ribbon to put back inside.
- Have older kids help younger ones, this one is great for sibling play.
- Older kids can practice knot tying while tying ribbons together for you.

Your Notes:

_____

_____

_____

_____

_____

PEELING TAPE

Materials:
- Packing tape
- Optional small toys

Directions:
Cut off pieces of tape 2 to 3 inches of length. Fold a little bit of the tape over on one end for better grabbing, stick your tape to the table surface or even on a door. Show your child how fun it is to peel tape off.

Tape down small toys! Your child will have to remove the tape before they can get the toy.

Heather:
It's funny how kids love the simplest things. Harvey got very excited about this activity! He practiced vocab by saying "stuck!", and really liked the cool sound it made when the tape came up.

He used both hands, sometimes at the same time, to pull up simple strips. He also had a lot of fun pulling up toys, and then played with them.

Bonus:
This is the perfect activity for when you are trying to work at your desk or are on a phone call and your little one is pestering you.

Tips/Variations:
- Be careful not to let them put the tape in their mouth and chew on it.
- Make it harder or easier by pressing it down or leaving a corner up.
- Get various colors of electrical tape for more fun and visual stimulation.

Bigger Kids/As They Grow:
- After they pull up the tape, have them stick it on the edge of the table.
- Lay down the tape in shapes or pictures and practice saying the names of the shapes, observe how they change as they pull up strips and/or rearrange them.
- Let your child help you lay down the tape.
- Let older kids tape down toys for the little ones. If they get really into it, it could occupy several kids for awhile.
- Give them several different colors of electrical tape and let them get creative laying it down.

Your Notes:
_____
_____
_____
_____
_____

TOWEL HOLDER & ROLLS

Materials:
- Kitchen Towel Holder
- Cardboard tubes

Directions:

Cut the cardboard tube into strips. Give the activity to your child.

Most children will get that the items go onto the kitchen towel holder if not show them and they soon pick it up.

Heather:
This one was super simple for Harvey and he just tossed them all on one handed and very quickly. I love the idea of just grabbing the paper towel holder though, and you could easily make this into a much more challenging game by turning into a ring toss.

For younger one year olds it will be more challenging and engaging to simply take them on and off.

Bonus:
Repurposing and reusing!

Tips/Variations:
- Make it harder by having them drop or toss the rings onto the stick.
- Color the strips and mention color names as you play.
- Hold or prop the towel holder sideways as the kids slide the rings on.

Bigger Kids/As They Grow:
- Toss the rings from farther and farther back.
- Kids can help cut and decorate the rings.
- Mark rings with numbers and toss or place them on in numerical order.
- Color rings the colors of the rainbow and put on in rainbow order while practicing color names.

Your Notes:

_____

_____

_____

_____

_____

DRAWING TRAY

Materials:

- Tray
- Oats

Directions:

Add enough oats to the tray that it makes a thin layer. Show your child how lines and shapes can be drawn by tracing with your fingers through the oats.

To reset the oats gently shake the tray.

Heather:
Harvey almost immediately put some in his mouth and I was happy that it was OK! He kept tasting little bits throughout the playtime and I had to get him some water as it made his throat a little dry, but he was enjoying it. He really loved the sensory sensation of the oats and he liked picking up and dropping pieces and running them through his fingers.

We brought out toy animals and they "ate" the oats, while we practiced animal names and sounds, then piled oats over them and dug them out.

Bonus:
It was excellent memory and focus practice teaching him to keep it on the tray.

Tips/Variations:
- Play with toy animals, making noises and sounds and feeding them.
- Play with toy cars and trucks, making tracks and moving oats around in dumptrucks, etc.
- Bury items or your or the child's hands.
- Use paint brushes or make-up brushes to move the oats around.
- Scoop the oats up high and let them fall back to the tray or over hands or objects.
- Draw shapes and letters using fingers.

Bigger Kids/As They Grow:
- Can hide items like large buttons and find them only by touch.
- Draw shapes and letters using a small stick.

Your Notes:

_____

_____

_____

_____

_____

FINGER PAINTING

Materials:

- Flour
- Food Coloring
- Containers for mixing

Directions:

Add 1/2 cup hot water to a bowl. Add in 1/4 cup of flour and mix with a whisk. Separate a spoonful of mix into however many colors you would like to create. Add 1 or 2 drops food coloring and mix thoroughly. Once the finger paint has cooled set up the paint as well as paper for the child to get creating with.

Nicolette:
I use painters' tape to tape down the sides of the paper to the table. This helps the little ones with paper that keeps moving!

Heather:
Harvey was a bit freaked out by the mess on his hands, prompting Nicolette to bring out some paintbrushes, which he liked better. Her kids, who obviously had more practice, really liked it, so I think after another time or two Harvey might get into it more. I love how Nicolette taped the papers down - it keeps not only the paper but also the kids from moving around too much. Kids of all ages love this one.

Bonus:
It was really visually stimulating for the kids (and me!) as the paint colors swirled and blended together very beautifully on the plate as we dipped into them.

Tips/Variations:
- If your child is not too thrilled with the concept of finger painting add some paint brushes and try finger painting another day.
- After painting with the individual colors, try mixing and swirling them.
- Do handprints.
- Use sponges or stamps to mark on the paper.
- Paint on a sidewalk or rock wall.

Bigger Kids/As They Grow:
- Name the colors as you paint.
- Make the paints only in primary colors and mix them to see what colors they will make.
- Use many hues of only one color in a session. Do a different color each time.
- Make stamps of leaves or rocks and enjoy the marks they make.

Your Notes:

_____

_____

_____

_____

MESS FREE PAINT EXPLORING

Materials:
- Ziplock bag
- Thick tape
- Colorful paints
- Cardstock

Directions:
Measure the cardstock in the ziplock bag and cut to size. Place blobs of paint on the cardstock and slip the cardstock into the ziplock. Zip it closed pushing most of the air out.

Tape the ziplock closed with your thick tape to prevent leaks. Tape the paint bag to your table or in a tray for your child to enjoy all day long!

Show your child how the paints are moved with fingers and eventually mixed.

Heather:
This one might take a few introductions to get your child interested. Harvey found it interesting but didn't quite get it at first. We had it taped to a tray that was on the floor, and first he pretended to eat it and we all had a good laugh, then he got up and stood on it.

I moved the paint around a little to show him what to do, and he tried a little, but he still wanted me to do it for him.

Bonus:
When I taped it to the kids' table at home and left it there for a few days, he did occasionally go visit it and play with it. The older kids loved it and wanted their own. It's very nice for visual stimulation.

Tips/Variations:
- Use both light and dark colors for best visual contrast.
- Make sure to keep sharp objects away.

Bigger Kids/As They Grow:
- This is a nice quiet activity that older kids can get absorbed in occasionally.
- Try out different color schemes.
- Name colors.

Your Notes:

_____

_____

_____

_____

_____

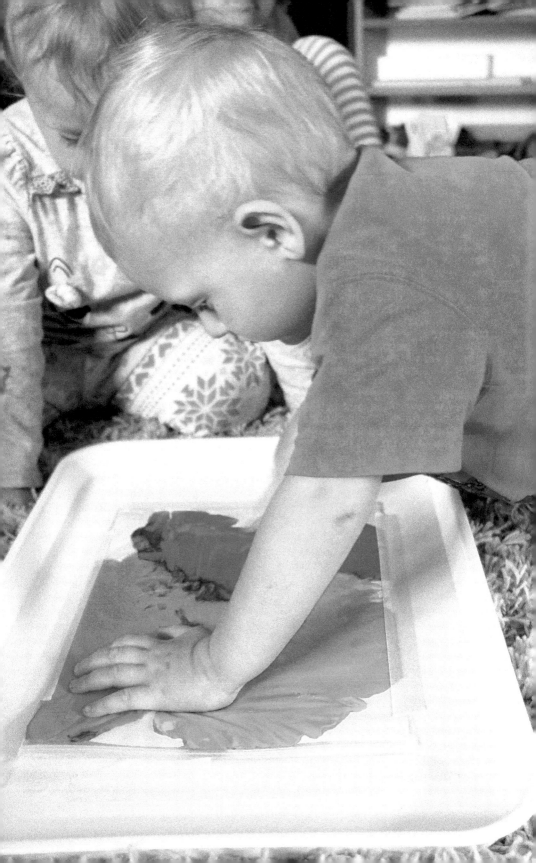

SENSORY BOTTLES

Materials:

- Clear bottle with lid
- Items that are water resistant, pom poms, beads, buttons
- Foods coloring
- Optional glitter
- Glue / hot glue gun

Directions:

Once your bottle is clean, add your items in. You will want something that floats and something that sinks. Example pom poms and beads. Now fill the bottle with water and add one drop of your choice of coloring. Use your glue to secure the lid to prevent leaks and little ones from opening it.

Show your child how moving the bottle around will make the items float and sink. Cause and effect. Such fun!

Nicolette:
I love using sensory and discovery bottles with toddlers. It allows them to interact with items that would normally be a no no for them, such as beads, which are small and a choking hazard.

Heather:
Harvey was very pleased by the sensory bottle, and sat happily holding it for quite some time. It helps build upper body gross motor skills and strength when they hold it up and shake it and it's a nice chance to practice some vocabulary like up and down, side to side, and sink and float.

Bonus:
It's also just really fun to look at, for both kids and mom.

Tips/Variations:
- You can set it on a table at their eye level and turn it over and over if it's too heavy for them or they get tired of holding it.
- Great for car rides.
- You can make similar bottles with different colored waters.
- You can make it an active toy by having them copy movements you show them while they are holding it (shaking in different directions, holding it out, up, etc.). This also helps with language skills.

Bigger Kids/As They Grow:
- Even older kids and adults love these, they're very soothing.
- Older kids can help make the sensory bottles. My daughter loves making glitter ones.

Your Notes:

_____

_____

_____

_____

_____

FOAM SENSORY BOTTLE

Materials:

- Clear bottle with lid
- Liquid dish soap
- Glitter

Directions:

Fill your bottle until it is ¼ full of water. Add in a squirt of dish soap as well as some glitter. Use glue to secure the lid to the sensory bottle.

Now shake the bottle and see how it makes tons of foam!

Heather:
This sensory bottle is mesmerizing, very fun to look at. Harvey and I enjoyed playing with the bottle and looking at it for quite a while while Nicolette and I chatted.

He did want to open it, so make sure you glue the lid down. It's great for visual stimulation.

Bonus:
This bottle is very soothing, great for calming a fussy child. Or a tired mother.

Tips/Variations:
- Leave the bottle on a counter to settle and see how the glitter looks like it is suspended in the air as the foam bubbles pop and disappear.

Bigger Kids/As They Grow:
- Older kids will love this bottle as well.
- Older kids can help make the bottles.

Your Notes:

_____

_____

_____

_____

_____

DRY SENSORY BOTTLES

Materials:
- Clear bottle with lid
- Color rice
- Paper clips or other interesting items
- Optional: Large child safe magnet

Color Rice Materials:
- 4 Small ziplock
- 1/3 cup Rice X 4
- 4 teaspoons of Vinegar
- Wax paper
- Food coloring

Directions:
To make 4 colors of color rice add 1/3 cup of rice to each of the 4 ziplocks. Add in 1 teaspoon of vinegar to each of the 4 ziplock bags as well as 3 drops of your choice of food coloring to each bag.

Press the air out of the ziplock and zip closed. Rub the rice in the bag until all the color is mixed in with the rice. Empty your damp rice out on a sheet of wax paper to air dry. Optionally bake for a few minutes to dry.

Add your color rice to the sensory bottle and any items you are looking to use as well. We have used paperclips to make this an extendable activity as the child grows. The younger children will be delighted at the sound the colorful rice makes and the older children will be fascinated with the magnetic properties of the paper clips and magnets.

Heather:
It took a while to get Harvey interested. Eventually, I began rolling the bottle back and forth on the table and he was attracted to the sound. He then rolled it around and shook it for quite a while. He eventually used the magnet as well to move the paper clips around though I don't think he exactly understands the cause and effect just yet. My four year old however, understood and really got into it. He was very fascinated by the magnets and didn't want to put them down.

Bonus:
Between my toddler and my 4 year old I got quite a bit of mileage out of this one. You can also reuse the rice for other activities.

Tips/Variations:
- Use high quality dyes in bright colors for the best effect.
- To freshen up the activity you can change out or add different small magnetic objects.

Bigger Kids/As They Grow:
- Older kids will enjoy helping you color the rice.
- Use the opportunity to learn about magnets in books or online.

Your Notes:

_____

_____

_____

_____

OOBLECK

Materials:

- 2 cups water
- 3 to 4 cups cornstarch
- Small amount of food coloring (optional)

Directions:

Start with the water in the bowl and add the cornstarch cup by cup stirring until it has a gooey consistency. You might have to use your hands at this point. Pour the mix out into a large plastic dish for the kids to play with.

Oobleck is both gooey and crumbly at the same time depending on what kind of pressure you apply. Children can slap (try make a splash) and it goes hard whereas when they try to make an imprint with say a hand the hand will sink into the oobleck. It truly is a fascinating sensory experience.

Heather:
This activity is pure fun for the whole family. Nicolette has a really large shallow bin, so there were 6 of us around the table playing with it together for at least 20 minutes straight. It is such a cool sensory feeling, you can't even really describe it. Harvey was mesmerized, along with the rest of us. We made it in a really pretty lavender color that was nice too. We loved dripping it on each others hands and sinking our hands into it. It was one of the most fun things I've done in a long time. I was so glad my four year old was there as well. Don't be intimidated by making Oobleck, it's well worth at least trying!

Bonus:
It's a good chance to practice memory and self control skills with your toddler, guiding them to keep it over the tray or bowl or whatever you use, but you can still be relaxed about it because any drips just turn back to powder and are easily cleaned up and wash right off of clothes.

Tips/Variations:
- Make various colors by adding color to the water before adding the cornstarch.
- Add a few drops of essential oils or extracts, or a few teaspoons of spices for a further sensory experience.
- Try matching colors and scents, like red oobleck with cherry or strawberry extract, or purple with grape. (Don't forget this is taste safe!)
- For a corn-free sensory material you can substitute tapioca starch in the same ratio.

Bigger Kids/As They Grow:
- Bigger kids may want to help you make oobleck, or suggest ideas for colors or scents.

Your Notes:

_____

_____

_____

_____

_____

PEEK A BOO BOOK

Materials:
- Picture board book
- Post-its

Directions:
Add new life to your child's favorite picture book. Place post-its over the images and play peek a boo with them!

Heather:
I love the brilliant simplicity of this idea, as toddlers love lift the flap books but often end up ripping the flaps off. We had tons of fun doing this with an animal book and practicing animal names.

Bonus:
Older kids love it too and can even place flaps for the younger ones and look at the books with them. Great for trips when you can only take a few books with you!

Tips/Variations:
- Start by only partially covering a single picture and see if your child can guess what it will be. After a few readings, cover up the item completely and see if they remember what it is.
- Work with your toddler on pulling up the flap without removing it from the book. This is great fine motor practice.
- Just let them pull the flaps off however they want, and place them back on if they want to.

Bigger Kids/As They Grow:
- Alternate the placement of the post-its so that some should be lifted up to see under them, some should be pulled down, and others pulled back from the sides.
- Depending on the child, cover an area with a few or several items underneath it. Let them peek for 5 or 10 seconds then see how many items they can remember.

Your Notes:

_____

_____

_____

_____

The 2nd little rubber A s

FISHING FISH

Materials:

- Printable fish -> www.powerfulmothering.com/ideas1/
- Cardstock
- Paperclips
- Punch
- Magnetic pole

Directions:

Print out the fish on cardstock and cut them out. Laminate them and then use a punch to make holes and attach the paper clips to the fish.

Place the fish on your floor / carpet and let the fishing begin! This activity greatly increases hand eye co-ordination.

Heather:

This one was interesting as it took Harvey quite a while to get around to actually doing the activity. First he took a fish and ran around outside with it and so did Nicolette's kids. They wanted to play with the fish.. This was ok, because Nicolette had laminated it, which I highly recommend.

But then when he did get interested, the other kids wouldn't let him have the fishing pole as they were enjoying it too much! Then we played a few variations. Finally, Harvey did the activity as intended. He really had to concentrate and experiment with it a bit, but was quite successful and happy about it.

Bonus:

This is a great family game that all the children loved.

Tips/Variations:

- The adult can attach the fish to the magnet on the pole and hold it in the air. The child can take the fish off of the magnet and put it back on.
- Put the fish in a basket or bucket.
- Count the fish as you take them out.
- Laminate the fish and let your child hold and play with them.

Bigger Kids/As They Grow:

- Try to get multiple fish or just one at a time, whichever is harder.
- Pretend to throw the fish back or fry it and eat it. (Pretend play)
- Count the fish and talk about the colors.

Your Notes:

_____
_____
_____
_____
_____

STICKERS

Materials:

- Sheet of stickers about the size of your thumbnail
- Paper

Directions:

Stickers are a great intro to more delicate fine motor control. Either pass the stickers one by one to your child or have them remove stickers from the sticker sheet themselves and place on the paper.

Nicolette:
I always remove the sticker paper around the stickers with gives more of an edge for children to grip on.

Heather:
Both Harvey and my four year old were immediately engaged and enjoying themselves. It was fun watching Harvey struggle with it a little bit with a super cute look of concentration on his face. Sometimes he turned to me to help get them off of his finger, but much of the time he did it on his own.

Nicolette helped him get the stickers off the backing when he needed it. The small size stickers require very small finger movements, amazing for development (and doesn't feel as wasteful to me). I think he would have kept going with it all day if we'd let him.

Bonus:
It was a very nice quiet time and Nicolette and I were able to have a chat as we assisted the kids.

Tips/Variations:
- If your stickers are in rows fold the sticker paper over so that half of the stickers are exposed for the child to grip on.

Bigger Kids/As They Grow:
- Draw on or print out pages with circle or shape outlines for them to place the stickers on.

Your Notes:

_____

_____

_____

_____

_____

ROLL BALL KNOCK OVER

Materials:

- Plastic bottles (spice bottles, cold drink bottles)
- Ball

Directions:

Set up your bottles next to each other. Encourage your child to roll the ball towards the bottles to knock them over.

Start close to the bottles and over time get further and further away from them to allow for more of a challenge.

Heather:

I only had to demonstrate this for Harvey once and it sure got his attention quickly! It involves more participation than some of the activities as you have to keep setting up the bottles, but his enjoyment in knocking them down made it well worth it.

Bonus:

I actually got to use some of the spice bottles I've been saving for so long.

Tips/Variations:

- Experiment with different size and weight of balls.
- The activity can be extended by playing with and stacking the bottles.
- Try doing this in different locations around the house and outside to mix it up.

Bigger Kids/As They Grow:

- Older kids can help you and your toddler by being bottle stackers and ball retrievers.
- Older children will love to play this game as well, let them try when the baby tires of it.

Your Notes:

_____

_____

_____

_____

_____

SENSORY STICKS

Materials:
- Jumbo craft sticks
- Hot glue gun
- Sensory materials such a pom poms, ribbons, buttons, feathers, felt, sand-paper, pipe cleaners etc

Directions:
Hot glue your materials onto the jumbo craft stick to make them secure for little ones to explore.

Nicolette:
I love to give items like this in a basket for the little ones to pick out as they like. Show them each one commenting on the texture or color to help expand those vocabulary words.

Heather:
Harvey was interested in these right away.He was calling the pompoms on the stick "bubbles," which I thought was cute and showed me insight into his vocab and thinking processes.

He liked this activity as an interactive one, sitting on my lap and showing me the sticks and "talking" about them. He was actually interested in them longer than I thought he would be, so I found this activity a success.

Bonus:
Find a little bag to keep them in and bring it when you want to go try to visit with another adult or you have to sit and wait somewhere to keep your child happier and calmer (maybe!).

Tips/Variations:
- Add sticks as you get inspiration in daily life.
- Use the sticks to practice vocabulary, simply by talking to your child about them as he or she explores it.

Bigger Kids/As They Grow:
- Place one or a couple of sticks in a bag or under a blanket and see if they can identify which stick it is only by feel.

Your Notes:

_____

_____

_____

_____

_____

SHAKER BOTTLES

Materials:

- Spice bottle or similar
- Noise making fillers, Straws, jingle bells, beads
- Glue
- Optional washi tape for decoration

Directions:

Clean up your bottle. Make sure your bottle is dry and then add your noise making fillers. Use your glue / hot glue to secure the lid of the bottle to avoid unintentional opening.

Use the optional washi tape to add a decorative touch. Shake shake shake!

Heather:
Another favorite. It's like a rattle, but with visual stimulation, and you don't have to worry about it getting lost at the grocery store as you can easily make more.

It's nice to just take with you everywhere you go or keep it out at home. Never know when it'll come in handy as a distraction. Harvey has been using this shaker for weeks now. He even took it into the bath the other day. I love it.

Bonus:
The day we made this shaker, my four year old fell down on our way home and was overly upset and crying more than usual. As I was holding him I started shaking the bottle near his ear just to give him a distracting noise and it helped.

Tips/Variations:
- Put a variety of items, some shiny and colorful, and some natural materials like pinecones and shells.
- Do themed shakers with items of all one color.
- Bring this along in the car or wherever you go for an easy distraction.

Bigger Kids/As They Grow:
- Older kids will love looking for items to put in the shaker.
- Older kids can use the shaker to help soothe younger ones.
- Make shakers like this and give them away as gifts. (Just make sure to glue the lid on very well.)

Your Notes:

_____

_____

_____

_____

_____

EXPLORING WITH OUR FEET

Materials:

- Bubble wrap
- Painters tape

Directions:

Tape bubble wrap to the floor with your painters' tape. Invite your child to step onto and then jump on the bubble wrap to hear the popping sounds.

Heather:

This is a fun rainy day activity and a great way to encourage jumping and hopping for your toddler, great for gross motor skills and coordination. What's not to like about jumping on bubble wrap? Lots of smiles with this activity.

Bonus:

You get to pop a few too! And that satisfying sound, haha!

Tips/Variations:

- Do this when older kids are not around to give your toddler a chance.
- Hold their hands for more stability if they need it.
- Pop a few to get them started, they may not know what to do right away.

Bigger Kids/As They Grow:

- Have them try hopping on only one foot or the other.

Your Notes:

_____

_____

_____

_____

_____

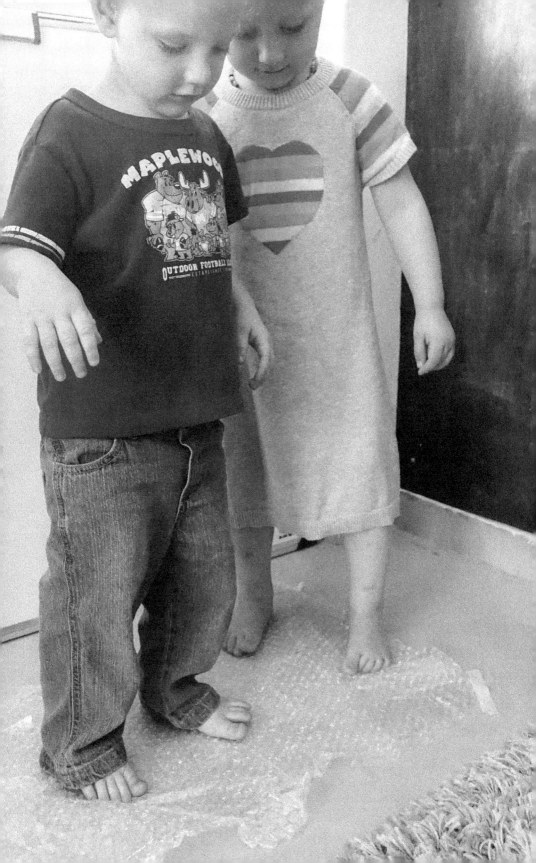

SILKY EXPLORE

Materials:

- Silk like scarves or similar
- Optional basket

Directions:

Place scarves into the basket or simply in a pile on the floor. Invite your child to feel and explore the scarves. Rub their skin to feel the silky texture, throw it up in the air and watch it float down.

Some children will lay on the floor and cover themselves in it while others enjoy the visual input from looking through the different color materials.

Heather:
Nicolette had a bunch of very light, brightly colored scarves that were perfect for this activity. Most of the scarves I own are bigger and heavier, so I will be keeping my eyes open for light, inexpensive, smaller scarves, as I've always wanted to have a little scarf basket like this one for the kids!

This is so great for just sitting on the floor and playing, with other moms and other kids as well. Part of what's fun with these is the interaction, so enjoy it with your toddler, relax and get silly!

Bonus:
It's a fun and relaxing activity for the mom also, and you have a reason to bring beautiful materials into your home (instead of plastic junk)!

Tips/Variations:
- Hide objects amongst the scarves in the basket to make a hide and seek game.

Bigger Kids/As They Grow:
- How high can you toss the scarf?
- How small can you fold the scarf?
- Color sort or make a rainbow of scarves.

Your Notes:

_____

_____

_____

_____

_____

BEAN BAG PLAY

Materials:

- 4 Bean Bags
- Basket

DIY Bean Bag Materials:

- Beans / Lentils / Popcorn
- Felt
- Hot glue gun

Directions:

Cut to size 2 sheets of felt. Hot glue 3 sides closed with a seam allowance so that your fingers do not touch the hot glue. Stuff the pocket with your choice of material and hot glue the remaining seam closed. Trim excess felt if needed on the edges.

The aim of this game is for Mom to toss the bean bag into the basket and for the child to retrieve it. You can also mix it up and take turns throwing the bean bags into the basket.

Heather:

Bean bag fun is so simple and perfect for kids this age. The possibilities for these bean bags for all ages is endless. They are the perfect size and weight for tossing without anyone getting hurt.

Bonus:

I actually made my own bean bags at home, and decorated them, in less than 10 minutes. They look like they were bought at the store! This is new crafty heights for me. You can do it, ladies!!

Tips/Variations:

- Place the bean bags on the child's back and have them crawl around until it falls off. It's a great way to burn energy indoors.
- Let your child stack them on your head.
- Simply toss the bags back and forth to each other.

Bigger Kids/As They Grow:

- Races are great if they are a bit older and there are other kids around. Place the bean bags on their backs or heads and let them go.
- Use the "monster" from the Feed the Monster game (page 106) and try to toss the beanbags into the mouth.
- Make sets, with 2 or 3 each of a few different colors. Have tossing contests to knock down light blocks or empty cans or whatever you find around the house to stack, or aim at a basket. It makes for great family time and improves older kids' motor skills as well.

Your Notes:

_____

_____

_____

_____

_____

UNWRAPPING GAME

Materials:
- Sheet of wrapping paper
- Smallish toy

Directions:
Fold or roll the toy up inside the wrapping paper. Do not use tape. Ask the child what they think is inside. Let them unwrap it. Be excited about finding the toy with your child.

Rewrap the toy in front of them and ask them again to guess what is inside. Repeat this until the child tires of it.

Heather:
This one is amazing for its simplicity and ability to keep a toddler interested for a long period of time when you are near. It's effortless extendable play as they will likely play with the toy after the paper fun is done. It's a fun way to hang out with your toddler, with opportunities for multi-tasking.

Bonus:
I've already been able to pass Harvey off to my husband and my other kids while playing this game.

Tips/Variations:
- Use small toy animals and vehicles and you get in lots of vocab and noises.
- You don't have to use a huge piece of wrapping paper, if you can roll the toy a few times, that's enough.

Bigger Kids/As They Grow:
- Kids of all ages love to give and this is a fun one for older siblings to do with younger ones.

Your Notes:

_____

_____

_____

_____

_____

MARACAS

Materials:

- Plastic easter eggs
- Large plastic spoons
- Tape or washi tape
- Lentils / rice / beans / straws / anything that can make a noise inside the egg.
- Optional glue

Directions:

Add a bit of your prefered filling into the egg. The egg should make a nice rattle type sound when shaken. Tape or glue the egg closed. Place the egg between the 2 spoons and use tape to secure them together. Use more tape at the base of the 2 spoons to secure the handle.

Have fun with your child and their new musical instrument!

Heather:
These make such a great noise, just loud enough, not too loud! It's much more fun to make enough for yourself, all small kids in your house, and for both hands if possible, as all will be attracted.

This one is very fun for social and controllable active indoor play (but Harvey also lay down for a few minutes playing with one too). I naturally came up with lots of ideas to extend the play, but we also all just sat around shaking them and smiling at each other while enjoying the sound! There's something therapeutic about it.

Bonus:
Repurpose all those empty plastic easter eggs instead of letting them float around the house until they get cracked and then throwing them away.

Tips/Variations:
- Sing or put on some music and shake and dance.
- Let them hit it on a soft object like a pillow.
- Parade around the house or in a circle while shaking.

Bigger Kids/As They Grow:
- Sing or put on some music and practice shaking in time.
- Tap out and practice rhythms on a pillow or couch cushion.

Your Notes:

_____

_____

_____

_____

_____

JINGLE BRACELETS

Materials:

- Pipe cleaner
- Jingle bells

Directions:

Measure the size of your child's arm and make sure you can remove the pipe cleaner over their hand. String some bells on the pipe cleaner and close off the pipe cleaner by wrapping it around itself.

Slip the new jingle bracelet over your child's hand and watch the shaking and dancing fun!

Heather:

My kids think that jewelry made of pipe cleaners is the coolest thing in the world, so this was a natural win for Harvey. He loved shaking the bells, and we did some dancing and shaking.

Bonus:

Make a matching anklet and stomp around!

Tips/Variations:

- When your child tires of wearing it hang it on a door in the house, like the bathroom or the front door where they can enjoy looking at it and hearing the noise.
- Make a bracelet for yourself and other members of the family and have a jingle dance party.
- Hide the bracelet in a basket underneath the materials in the Silky Explore Basket (page 94), making sure the ends are well folded so they don't catch and ruin the materials.
- Give the bracelet to your child when you are out and about and they get fussy and you need a distraction.

Bigger Kids/As They Grow:

- Bigger kids love to make things out of pipe cleaners. Let them make their own bracelets. They will probably make one for you too.

Your Notes:

_____

_____

_____

_____

_____

DUPLO & STICKS

Materials:

- 12 Craft sticks
- 4 Large Duplo bricks

Directions:

Set out the duplo bricks upside down. Show your child how the craft sticks fit into the holes of the bricks.

Heather:

I love this one. There are so many simple variations your child may do on his own, and all of them require fine motor movements and concentration. Harvey caught onto this one right away and enjoyed it.

Bonus:

A week after learning this activity, I needed to pacify my toddler for a few minutes while we waited on his brother to come out of the bathroom.

He was super fussy so I grabbed a few duplos off the floor and a few sticks from the bag up on the shelf and set them in front of us. He obviously remembered the activity and immediately started putting the sticks in the holes, and he stayed engaged in it as long as I needed him to. WIN!

Tips/Variations:

- Let them put the stick in different compartments of the legos.
- Add counting and color naming.

Bigger Kids/As They Grow:

- If your child is older try color matching or patterns.

Your Notes:

FEED THE MONSTER

Materials:

- Large plastic bottle
- Tape
- Large pom poms or buttons
- Marker pen

Directions:

Cut a large hole in the middle of your bottle large enough for your child to safely put their hand through. Use the tape to tape the edges of your mouth so that it doesn't hurt your child as they stick their hands in there. The color tape also makes the mouth more visible for children to feed the monster. Draw 2 eyes with your marker pen or glue 2 large googly eyes on.

Children will then feed the monster the pom poms one by one then fish them out to start again.

Heather:
This is one of my favorite activities in the book because it is SO easy, fun and versatile. Harvey immediately got the concept and of course loved not only tossing the pompoms in, but dumping them out, which is a cognitive challenge as the hole is in the middle of the side. There are many natural ways to extend and vary this play.

Bonus:
I made this at home and kids and I love it even though it looks like a Pinterest fail! I forgot about the tape around the mouth (oops - that's what this book is for!), my eyes look kind of mean, and I made the hole much lower than Nicolette had. Still, my kids and I have already had quite a bit of fun and I've used it to play with and occupy Harvey and my 4 year old several times. And I have some practice, so I'll make the next one better!

Tips/Variations:
- Use other items, like buttons or even the bean bags from the Beanbag Toss activity. Page 96.
- Use different sized bottles for traveling or to change things up.
- Leave the top off and also allow them to drop the poms through the top.
- Reach in the mouth and place a hand or toy dumptruck under the top, try to drop the pom onto it.
- Leave this game out for your kid to play with throughout the day on occasion. You will have occasional pompom cleanup though.

Bigger Kids/As They Grow:
- Older kids can play alongside or help the toddler, depending on their age.
- Can be turned into a tossing activity that can be adjusted to any skill level by placing the "Monster" on a higher surface and getting farther away.

Your Notes:

_____

_____

_____

_____

REFERENCES

ref1 - http://www.healthofchildren.com/G-H/Gross-Motor-Skills.html

ref2 - http://study.com/academy/lesson/what-are-fine-motor-skills-in-children-development-definition-examples.html

ref3 - http://study.com/academy/lesson/communication-skills-definition-examples.html

ref4 - http://www.learningrx.com/cognitive-definition-faq.htm

ref5 - www.cde.ca.gov/sp/cd/re/itf09socemodev.asp

ref6 - www.scholastic.com/parents/resources/article/creativity-play/endless-possibilities

RESOURCES

Looking for the items mentioned in this book? Pop on over to the resources page dedicated to this book.

http://www.powerfulmothering.com/ideas1/

INDEX

CPSIA information can be obtained
at www.ICGtesting.com
Printed in the USA
BVHW021811010620
580415BV00011B/362